Heartbound Odyssey:

Crafting Passion, Community, and the Game
Guide's Road Ahead

ELEANOR QUINN

Introduction
    Overview of Heartbound
    Brief History and Development Information
PART 1 Game Overview
    Genre and Platform
    Release Information
    Core Gameplay Features
Part 2 Narrative and Gameplay
    Storyline and Character Overview
    Gameplay Mechanics
    Choices and Consequences
Part 3 Alternate Reality Game (ARG)
    Cryptographic Puzzles and Lore
    Connection to the Main Game
Part 4 Combat System in Heartbound: An Artful
Dance of Skill and Strategy
    Skill-based Approach
    Equipment and Augmentations
    Unique Mini-games for Enemies
        Evolution and Community Engagement
Part 5
Embarking on the Heartbound Odyssey: A
Chronicle of Inspiration, Challenges, and Resilience
    Inspirations and Influences
    Greenlight, Kickstarter, and Early Access
    Challenges and Delays
Part 6
Heartbound's Ongoing Saga: Navigating Monthly

Updates, Beta Releases, and the Road Ahead

    Monthly Update Videos: A Window into Development

    Beta Releases and Development Progress

    Future Release Plans and Goals

        Evolution and Adaptation: Navigating the Unknown

Part 7:

Heartbound's Journey: Navigating the Tides of Reception and Controversies

    Alpha and Beta Reception: Riding the Waves of Positivity

    Comparisons with Undertale: Navigating Controversial Waters

    Recognition on Game Jolt: Riding the Crests of Success

Part 8

Building the Heartbound Guild: Crafting a Community Tapestry

    Guild Name and Theme: The Heartbeat of Community Identity

    Community Engagement Platforms: The Nexus of Connection

    In-Game and Out-of-Game Activities: Crafting Bonds Beyond Pixels

Conclusion:

    Summary of Heartbound's Journey:

    Anticipation for Future Releases:

Introduction

Heartbound, an emotionally charged role-playing video game developed by the American indie developer Pirate Software, has captured the hearts of gamers since its initial foray into the gaming scene. This introduction provides a comprehensive overview of Heartbound, offering a glimpse into its captivating narrative, unique gameplay mechanics, and the journey it has undertaken during its development.

Overview of Heartbound

Heartbound is not just another RPG; it is an immersive experience that delves into the profound emotions of its central character. The game follows the story of a young boy grappling with depression, anxiety, and fear as he embarks on a poignant journey in search of his loyal companion, Baron. Set in various locations, Heartbound introduces players to a narrative that dynamically changes based on their interactions with the environment, other characters, and the innovative combat system.

The game, which embraces the role-playing genre, stands out for its emphasis on player choice. Every decision made by the player, whether it's interacting with objects, engaging with non-playable characters (NPCs), or making seemingly inconsequential choices, has a lasting impact on the game's unfolding story. This unique design element not only adds depth to the gameplay but also fosters a sense of agency among players.

Brief History and Development Information

Heartbound's journey began with an alpha version released for Microsoft Windows, OS X, and Linux in November 2016, showcased on Steam Greenlight. Remarkably, the game gained overwhelming support from the gaming community, securing its position as a top game on the platform in a mere ten days. Following this success, a beta version hit the digital shelves in February 2017, accompanied by a triumphant Kickstarter crowdfunding campaign.

The Kickstarter campaign, launched on February 24, 2017, proved to be a resounding success, achieving its funding goal within the first 24 hours. By the campaign's conclusion on March 26, it had surpassed expectations, raising a noteworthy $19,272 against its initial $5,000 goal. With the backing of an enthusiastic community, Heartbound ventured into Steam early access on Christmas Day of 2018, unveiling the first two chapters: "Homeworld" and "The Tower."

Initially slated for a full release in December 2017, the game took a slightly different path. The developers opted for a segmented release approach, providing an early access version in December 2018 with plans to expand content gradually through patches. This decision aimed to allow players to engage with the evolving narrative and gameplay while the developers continued to refine and expand the Heartbound universe.

As the game progressed through its development phases, it faced its share of challenges, including the impact of the global COVID-19 pandemic. The increased scope resulting from the Kickstarter campaign's stretch goals, coupled with the personal challenges faced by the development team, led to delays. However, the team actively addressed concerns, offering monthly update videos starting in 2022 to keep the community informed and engaged.

The latest update, as of September 2023, indicated the beta version of Chapter 3, titled "Animus," was set for release on December 24, 2023, with a full game release anticipated in 2024. However, it's worth noting that the development process has been ongoing, and the beta version of Chapter 3 remains in partial release as of December 25, 2023.

In summary, Heartbound's journey from its humble beginnings on Steam Greenlight to its ongoing development showcases the dedication of the Pirate Software team and the unwavering support of the gaming community. This introduction sets the stage for a deeper exploration of Heartbound's gameplay, narrative intricacies, and the reception it has garnered in the gaming world.

PART 1 Game Overview

In the expansive realm of video games, Heartbound emerges as a distinctive gem, combining emotional storytelling with innovative gameplay. This section provides a detailed exploration of Heartbound's genre, supported platforms, its release trajectory, and the core gameplay features that make it a standout experience for players.

Genre and Platform

Heartbound is a role-playing video game that beckons players into a world where emotions intertwine with gameplay. Developed by Pirate Software, this indie RPG boasts a unique blend of narrative depth and interactive mechanics. The game primarily caters to players on Microsoft Windows and Linux platforms, providing a digital canvas for its emotionally charged odyssey.

The decision to focus on these platforms aligns with the game's indie roots, allowing for a more intimate connection between the developers and the player community. The choice of platforms reflects a commitment to accessibility, ensuring that a diverse range of gamers can partake in the emotional journey that Heartbound unfolds.

Release Information

Heartbound made its initial impact on the gaming landscape with an alpha version released in November 2016. This early glimpse showcased the game's potential, allowing players to experience its unique narrative and gameplay mechanics. The alpha version was made available on Microsoft Windows, OS X, and Linux, marking the first steps of Heartbound's journey toward becoming a fully-fledged gaming experience.

The game's progression continued with a beta release and a Kickstarter crowdfunding campaign in February 2017. The success of the campaign propelled Heartbound into Steam early access on Christmas Day of 2018. The initial release featured the first two chapters, "Homeworld" and "The Tower," giving players a taste of the emotional rollercoaster that awaited them.

While initially slated for a full release in December 2017, the development team opted for a different approach. The decision to release the game in sections through early access allowed for ongoing player engagement and feedback, shaping the evolving narrative and gameplay. This segmented release strategy demonstrated a commitment to delivering a polished and evolving experience, ensuring that each addition to the game was a carefully crafted piece of the larger puzzle.

As the development journey progressed, Heartbound encountered delays, notably due to the expanded scope resulting from the Kickstarter campaign's stretch goals and the unforeseen challenges posed by the global COVID-19 pandemic. The team, however, maintained open communication with the community through monthly update videos, fostering a sense of transparency and shared anticipation.

The latest development update, as of September 2023, outlined plans for the beta version of Chapter 3, titled "Animus," with a targeted release date of December 24, 2023. The full game release is projected for 2024, marking the culmination of years of dedication and creativity by the development team.

Core Gameplay Features

At the heart of Heartbound lies a set of core gameplay features that distinguishes it within the RPG landscape. The game's narrative-driven approach intertwines seamlessly with interactive elements, providing players with an immersive and emotionally charged experience.

1. Player Choice and Consequences:

   - Heartbound thrives on the concept of player agency. Every interaction, decision, and choice made by the player leaves a lasting imprint on the game world. The narrative dynamically adapts to these choices, offering multiple pathways and endings. This emphasis on player agency elevates the overall gaming experience, creating a sense of ownership over the unfolding story.

2. Skill-Based Combat System:

- Departing from traditional RPG norms, Heartbound introduces a skill-based combat system. Unlike systems based on levels and experience points, combat in Heartbound relies on player skill and strategy. Each enemy presents a unique mini-game, requiring players to master various mechanics. The absence of random battles and the avoidable nature of encounters based on player progression contribute to a tailored and engaging combat experience.

3. Environmental Interactivity:
- Heartbound extends the player's influence beyond character interactions and combat. Every action, from

interacting with objects to seemingly mundane activities like turning off a light-switch or taking out the trash, influences the game's world. The environment reacts dynamically to player choices, adding depth to the overall narrative. This unique design feature ensures that every player's experience is distinctive, fostering a sense of shared discovery within the gaming community.

4. Alternate Reality Game (ARG):
      - Heartbound goes beyond the confines of the gaming screen with an Alternate Reality Game (ARG). A series of cryptographic puzzles, accessible from the game's website, provides additional lore and an alternative narrative parallel

to the main game. This innovative approach extends the storytelling beyond traditional boundaries, inviting players to engage with the game in a multifaceted manner.

In summary, Heartbound's game overview encapsulates its genre-defying nature, the platforms it calls home, its unconventional release strategy, and the core gameplay features that collectively shape its identity. As players traverse through the emotionally charged landscape of Heartbound, these elements harmonize to create a gaming experience that transcends the boundaries of traditional role-playing games.

Part 2 Narrative and Gameplay

In the realm of video games, Heartbound stands as a testament to the seamless integration of compelling narrative and innovative gameplay. This section delves into the heart of Heartbound's experience, unraveling the intricacies of its storyline, introducing its central characters, exploring gameplay mechanics, and examining the profound impact of choices and consequences within the game's world.

Storyline and Character Overview

At the core of Heartbound lies a narrative that transcends the boundaries of typical gaming experiences. The game centers around a young boy navigating the tumultuous terrain of emotions—depression, anxiety, and fear—on a poignant journey to find his cherished companion, Baron. As players embark on this emotional odyssey, they traverse diverse and visually stunning locations, each intricately woven into the fabric of the game's overarching story.

The narrative unfolds dynamically, shaped by the player's choices, interactions with the environment, and engagements with other characters. The central character's struggles and triumphs mirror the complexities of real-life emotions, creating a profound and relatable connection for players. Heartbound is not merely a game; it is an interactive narrative that explores the depths of human emotion, inviting players to confront and navigate the intricacies of the human psyche.

Beyond the central protagonist, Baron, Heartbound introduces a cast of characters that contribute to the richness of the story. Each character is carefully crafted, bringing unique personalities, motivations, and challenges to the forefront. The interactions with these characters are not just waypoints in the game but opportunities for players to immerse themselves in the emotional tapestry that Heartbound weaves.

Gameplay Mechanics

Heartbound's gameplay mechanics are a testament to its departure from conventional RPG norms. Rather than relying on traditional systems of levels, experience points, and consumables, the game adopts a skill-based approach that places the onus on the player's abilities and strategic thinking. This departure from the norm fosters a sense of engagement and investment in the outcome of each encounter.

1. Interactive Choices:

- Central to Heartbound's gameplay is the concept of player agency. Every choice made by the player, whether in dialogue, interactions with objects, or reactions to specific events, has a tangible impact on the unfolding narrative. The game remembers and adapts to these choices, resulting in a dynamic storytelling experience where decisions matter.

2. Combat System:

- Heartbound introduces a combat system that is far from traditional. Eschewing random battles, the game presents each enemy encounter as a unique mini-game. The player's skill and mastery of these mini-games influence the outcome of battles. This approach not only adds an element of skill-based challenge but also reinforces the idea that combat is an integral part of the overall narrative.

3. Environmental Interactivity:

- The game extends interactivity beyond character-driven choices to the environment itself. Every action, whether it's forgetting to turn off a light-switch or choosing to engage with seemingly inconspicuous objects, ripples through the game world. This innovative design ensures that the player's experience is not confined to scripted events but is shaped by a myriad of subtle interactions.

4. Equipment and Augmentations:

- Equipment in Heartbound is not just a collection of stat-boosting items; it becomes an extension of the player's journey. Found throughout the game world, equipment augments the protagonist's damage and maximum health, influencing the player's approach to combat and exploration. This integration of equipment into the overall narrative enhances the sense of progression and personalization.

Choices and Consequences

Heartbound's narrative is not a linear path but a tapestry of choices and consequences, each contributing to the unique experience of every player. The impact of player decisions resonates across the game, shaping dialogue, encounters, and the overall environment. This emphasis on choice and consequence elevates Heartbound beyond a traditional RPG, transforming it into an evolving narrative where the player is an active participant.

1. Multiple Pathways and Endings:

   - The game unfolds with a branching narrative, offering players multiple pathways and endings. The choices made throughout the journey influence the direction of the story, providing a sense of replayability as players explore different facets of the narrative. This non-linear approach reinforces the idea that every player's experience is uniquely their own.

2. Community Engagement:

- The emphasis on choices extends beyond the individual player to the community. Heartbound's design encourages players to share their experiences, choices, and discoveries with one another. This communal aspect adds an extra layer to the gameplay, as players collectively unravel the intricacies of the game's narrative.

3. Emotional Impact: - Perhaps the most profound consequence of choices in Heartbound is the emotional impact on players. As the narrative unfolds based on their decisions, players find themselves emotionally invested in the protagonist's journey. Joy, sorrow, and

moments of introspection become shared experiences within the gaming community, creating a powerful connection between the virtual world and the real emotions of the players.

In conclusion, Heartbound's narrative and gameplay intricately weave together to create an experience that transcends the boundaries of traditional role-playing games. The emotionally charged storyline, coupled with innovative gameplay mechanics and a dynamic system of choices and consequences, establishes Heartbound as a standout example of how gaming can be a deeply personal and emotionally resonant journey.

Part 3 Alternate Reality Game (ARG)

In the expansive landscape of video game storytelling, Heartbound doesn't merely confine its narrative to the pixels on the screen; it extends its reach into the real world through an ingenious Alternate Reality Game (ARG). This section unveils the mysteries of Heartbound's ARG, delving into the realm of cryptographic puzzles, the lore they unveil, and the intriguing connection between this augmented reality and the main game itself.

Cryptographic Puzzles and Lore

Heartbound's ARG introduces players to a parallel dimension of puzzles and lore, existing beyond the confines of the main game. Cryptographic puzzles, a staple of ARGs, serve as gateways to additional layers of narrative and world-building. These puzzles are not mere brain teasers; they are intricate pieces of a larger narrative puzzle, encouraging players to sharpen their wits and embark on a journey that transcends the boundaries of traditional gaming.

The puzzles embedded within the ARG provide a multifaceted experience. They range from traditional ciphers and codes to more complex cryptographic challenges, inviting players to explore various realms of puzzle-solving. As players successfully decipher these enigmatic codes, they unlock fragments of lore that delve into the rich backstory of Heartbound. These additional layers of narrative add depth to the overarching storyline, creating a sense of discovery that goes beyond the main game's narrative.

The lore revealed through the ARG isn't mere supplementary material; it's an integral part of the Heartbound universe. These cryptographic puzzles serve as conduits to hidden histories, untold tales, and the interconnectedness of characters and events. Engaging with the ARG isn't just a side quest; it's a crucial exploration of the game's expansive lore, offering players a chance to become archaeologists of the Heartbound narrative.

Connection to the Main Game

What sets Heartbound's ARG apart is its seamless integration with the main game. Rather than existing in isolation, the ARG acts as a parallel narrative, weaving in and out of the player's journey within the main game. The connection between the two is more than thematic; it's structural, creating a symbiotic relationship that enriches the overall gaming experience.

1. Foreshadowing and Unlockable Content:

- Successfully navigating the cryptographic puzzles in the ARG can act as a form of foreshadowing for events within the main game. Certain revelations or hidden narratives uncovered through the ARG may serve as hints or previews of what players can expect in future updates or chapters of Heartbound. In this way, the ARG becomes a tool for both storytelling and community engagement.

2. Parallel Narratives:

- The lore unveiled in the ARG doesn't merely echo the main game's narrative; it runs in parallel, offering insights into characters, locations, and events that might be tangential to the central storyline. This parallelism allows players to explore facets of the Heartbound universe that may not be immediately apparent in the main game, adding layers of complexity to the overarching narrative.

3. Community Collaboration:

- The ARG encourages collaboration within the Heartbound community. As players tackle cryptographic puzzles, they often share insights, strategies, and solutions with one another. This collaborative effort mirrors the communal nature of gaming, where a shared sense of discovery becomes a bonding experience. The ARG fosters a unique form of player interaction, creating a virtual space where minds converge to unravel the mysteries laid out before them.

4. Unlockable Game Content:
- Beyond narrative insights, successfully completing segments of the ARG can unlock additional content within the main game. Whether it's exclusive items, hidden locations, or unique encounters, the ARG becomes a bridge between the digital and augmented realities of Heartbound. This integration not only rewards players for their puzzle-solving prowess but also reinforces the notion that the game's universe is dynamic and interconnected.

The ARG serves as an extension of the Heartbound experience, blurring the lines between fiction and reality. It challenges players to think beyond the conventional boundaries of gaming, transforming the act of solving puzzles into a form of interactive storytelling. The ARG isn't a mere diversion; it's an integral part of the Heartbound narrative, inviting players to explore the hidden recesses of the game world.

Evolution of the ARG: As Heartbound has evolved over the years, so too has its ARG. The puzzles have become more intricate, the lore more expansive, and the connection to the main game more nuanced. The developers have utilized the ARG as a dynamic tool for community engagement, periodically introducing new puzzles, challenges, and lore fragments. This ongoing evolution ensures that even long-time players remain engaged, with the promise of continual discovery.

The September 2023 update video, as of the last available information, hinted at the continued growth of the ARG alongside the development of the main game. This synchronization ensures that players can immerse themselves in a cohesive narrative experience, seamlessly transitioning between the challenges presented in the ARG and the emotionally charged journey within the main game.

In conclusion, Heartbound's Alternate Reality Game is a testament to the creativity and innovation of its developers. By incorporating cryptographic puzzles, rich lore, and a tangible connection to the main game, the ARG elevates the gaming experience. It transforms players into active participants in a narrative that extends beyond the pixels on the screen, inviting them to uncover the hidden truths of Heartbound's universe through the cerebral engagement of an augmented reality game.

Part 4 Combat System in Heartbound: An Artful Dance of Skill and Strategy

The combat system in Heartbound is not just a series of clashes and conflicts; it's a carefully crafted symphony that integrates skill, strategy, and an innovative approach to create a gameplay experience unlike any other. In this exploration, we'll delve into the intricacies of Heartbound's combat system, examining its skill-based approach, the role of equipment and augmentations, and the engaging world of unique mini-games designed for each enemy encounter.

Skill-based Approach

Departing from traditional RPG conventions, Heartbound's combat system adopts a skill-based approach that places the emphasis squarely on the player's abilities rather than relying on character levels and experience points. This departure from the norm adds an extra layer of engagement, turning each encounter into a dynamic challenge where quick thinking and nimble fingers are just as important as strategic planning.

1. Precision and Timing:

   - In the world of Heartbound, combat is an art form. Players must master the precise timing of attacks, blocks, and dodges to overcome adversaries. This precision-oriented approach adds a layer of complexity, as success in combat is determined by the player's skillful execution of moves rather than the statistical prowess of a character.

2. Adaptable Strategies:

- The skill-based nature of combat encourages players to develop adaptable strategies. With no reliance on fixed character progression, each encounter becomes an opportunity for experimentation and growth. Players may find success through different approaches, fostering a sense of personalization in combat styles and strategies.

3. Mastery through Practice:

- Mastery in Heartbound's combat is not handed out; it's earned through practice and perseverance. The game challenges players to continually refine their skills, creating a satisfying sense of progression as they become more adept at navigating the mini-games associated with each enemy. This commitment to skill development aligns with the game's overarching theme of personal growth and resilience.

Equipment and Augmentations

In the tapestry of Heartbound's combat, equipment and augmentations serve as essential threads, allowing players to weave their own narrative of empowerment and strategy. Rather than a mere collection of stat-boosting items, equipment becomes a tangible extension of the protagonist's journey, influencing both combat effectiveness and the overall narrative.

1. Impact on Damage and Health:

   - Equipment in Heartbound is not just about aesthetics; it directly impacts the protagonist's damage output and maximum health. Discovering and equipping new items becomes a strategic decision, shaping the player's approach to combat and exploration. The tangible impact of equipment ensures that each piece becomes a meaningful part of the protagonist's journey.

2. Narrative Integration:

- What sets Heartbound apart is the seamless integration of equipment into the overarching narrative. Each piece of equipment tells a story, whether it's a weapon discovered in a hidden location or armor earned through a challenging encounter. This narrative integration enhances the emotional connection between the player and the protagonist, transforming equipment into more than just tools of combat but into relics of the journey.

3. Personalization and Choice:

- The diverse array of equipment allows players to personalize the protagonist's combat style. Whether favoring high damage output, enhanced defense, or a balance of both, players can tailor their approach based on personal preferences. This element of choice extends beyond combat, providing a sense of agency in how the protagonist navigates the challenges presented by the game.

Unique Mini-games for Enemies

Heartbound's enemies aren't just adversaries to be conquered; they are dynamic elements within a larger system of unique mini-games. Each enemy encounter introduces a distinct set of challenges, requiring players to adapt and strategize in real-time. This bespoke approach to enemy design not only adds variety to the gameplay but transforms combat into a series of engaging puzzles waiting to be solved.

1. Diverse Challenges:

- No two enemy encounters in Heartbound are alike. Each adversary introduces a unique mini-game, presenting players with diverse challenges that go beyond traditional turn-based combat. From memory-based sequences to rhythm games, the mini-games are a testament to the developers' creativity and a nod to the idea that every battle is a distinct experience.

2. Integration with Lore:

- The mini-games aren't just gameplay mechanics; they are integral to the lore and narrative of Heartbound. The challenges presented during combat are often reflective of the characteristics and behaviors of the enemies themselves. This integration adds a layer of storytelling to each encounter, encouraging players to view combat not just as a mechanical necessity but as a means of uncovering the depths of the game's universe.

3. Avoidable Encounters: - Heartbound breaks free from the convention of random battles by making a significant portion of encounters avoidable. The player's progression and choices influence the enemies they face,

contributing to a sense of agency in shaping the overall experience. This non-linear approach to encounters complements the game's theme of choice and consequence, ensuring that combat is not just a series of obligatory engagements but an intentional and dynamic part of the narrative.

Evolution and Community Engagement

As Heartbound has evolved over the years, the combat system has undergone refinement and expansion. The introduction of new chapters and updates brings with it not only additional challenges but also a commitment to community engagement.

Developers actively listen to player feedback, using it to fine-tune existing mechanics and introduce new elements that resonate with the community.

The September 2023 update video, as of the last available information, hinted at the ongoing development of Chapter 3, titled "Animus," showcasing new challenges and mini-games for players to explore. This commitment to evolution ensures that Heartbound's combat system remains a dynamic and engaging component of the overall gaming experience.

In conclusion, Heartbound's combat system is a testament to the developers' dedication to crafting an immersive and engaging gameplay experience. The skill-based approach, integration of equipment into the narrative, and the world of unique mini-games for enemies collectively contribute to a combat system that transcends the traditional boundaries of RPGs. As players traverse the emotionally charged landscape of Heartbound, the combat system becomes not just a series of challenges to overcome but a deeply woven part of the game's narrative tapestry.

Part 5

Embarking on the Heartbound Odyssey: A Chronicle of Inspiration, Challenges, and Resilience

The journey of Heartbound, an indie role-playing game developed by Pirate Software, is not just a chronicle of code and pixels but a tale of inspiration, community support, and the resilience of a dedicated development team. In this exploration, we'll traverse the development landscape of Heartbound, from the initial seeds of inspiration to the challenges faced, including the

Greenlight and Kickstarter phases, and the subsequent journey through Early Access.

Inspirations and Influences

Every great journey begins with inspiration, and Heartbound is no exception. The mind behind the game, Jason Thor Hall, drew influence from a diverse array of sources. Classics like Secret of Mana, EarthBound (and the Mother series), Wario Ware, Secret of Evermore, and the enigmatic 1057 all played a part in shaping the vision of Heartbound. This eclectic mix reflects not only a deep appreciation for the classics of the RPG genre but also a desire to push the boundaries and explore new dimensions of storytelling and gameplay.

These inspirations served as guiding stars, influencing everything from the narrative design to the gameplay mechanics. The result is a game that pays homage to its predecessors while carving out a unique identity, a delicate balance that few games achieve.

Greenlight, Kickstarter, and Early Access

The journey of Heartbound took a significant step forward with its debut on Steam Greenlight in December 2016. The response from the gaming community was nothing short of phenomenal, as the game garnered enough support to secure its place as a top game on the platform within a mere ten days. This swift success on Greenlight marked the beginning of a journey that would soon extend beyond mere anticipation to active community engagement.

Buoyed by the positive reception on Greenlight, Pirate Software launched a Kickstarter campaign on February 24, 2017. The goal was to secure funding for the development of the game and provide backers with an opportunity to contribute to the realization of Heartbound's vision. The campaign, fueled by the passion of the gaming community, achieved its funding goal within the first 24 hours, exceeding expectations and concluding on March 26, 2017, with a total of $19,272 raised against the initial $5,000 goal.

The Kickstarter success not only secured the financial backing needed for Heartbound's development but also galvanized a community of supporters. Backers weren't just investors; they became integral parts of the Heartbound journey, contributing ideas, feedback, and a shared enthusiasm for the game's potential.

With the wind of community support at its back, Heartbound ventured into Steam Early Access on Christmas Day of

2018. This marked a pivotal moment, as players finally got to experience the first chapters of the game, titled "Homeworld" and "The Tower." The decision to release the game in sections through Early Access wasn't just a practical one; it was a conscious effort to involve the community in the evolving narrative, allowing for feedback and iterative development.

Challenges and Delays

As any ambitious undertaking goes, Heartbound faced its share of challenges and unexpected twists in the development journey. The increased scope brought on by the Kickstarter campaign's stretch goals and unforeseen obstacles, such as the impact of the global COVID-19 pandemic, led to delays in the game's progress.

The challenges weren't just technical; they were personal. Members of the development team faced health issues, with some grappling with the effects of COVID-19 in early 2020. These hurdles could have derailed a less determined team, but Pirate Software, true to their name, sailed through the storm. To assuage concerns and maintain transparency, the team began releasing monthly update videos in 2022, providing insights into the development process and assuring the community that Heartbound was very much alive and kicking.

The commitment to transparency wasn't just a gesture; it was a lifeline for the community. As concerns grew about the prolonged development process, the monthly update videos served as beacons of reassurance. The developers acknowledged the challenges, shared the progress made, and outlined the road ahead. This open communication fostered a sense of trust and solidarity within the Heartbound community.

In the September 2023 update video, published on October 21, 2023, Jason Thor Hall shared the latest developments. The beta version of Chapter 3, titled "Animus," was set for release on December 24, 2023, with the full game release anticipated in 2024. This timeline, while indicative of the extended development journey, was met with understanding and support from a community that had weathered the storms alongside the development team.

Community Resilience and Anticipation

Through the challenges and delays, the Heartbound community stood resilient. The game's alpha and beta releases were met with enthusiasm, with IGN and Game Skinny expressing interest in the game's direction. The community engagement extended beyond gameplay, as players shared their experiences, theories, and excitement for what the future chapters held.

Heartbound's success wasn't just measured in funding milestones; it was reflected in the community's unwavering anticipation. On October 3, 2018, the game was in second place for the top indie release on Game Jolt. Fast forward to January 1, 2024, and Heartbound claimed the top spot, a testament to the enduring excitement and anticipation surrounding the game.

The community's resilience and support played a crucial role in navigating the challenges faced during the development journey. The developers reciprocated this support with a commitment to quality and a dedication to delivering an experience that would live up to the expectations of the Heartbound faithful.

Looking Ahead: The Ongoing Odyssey

As of the last available information, the beta version of Chapter 3, "Animus," was partially released on December 25, 2023, and remained in development. The full game release was projected for 2024, marking the next chapter in the ongoing odyssey of Heartbound.

The journey of Heartbound is not just a linear progression; it's an evolving narrative that continues to unfold. The challenges faced, the delays endured, and the unwavering support of the community have all become integral chapters in the story of Heartbound. The anticipation for the full release remains palpable, fueled by the shared enthusiasm of a community that has weathered the storm and emerged stronger.

In conclusion, the development journey of Heartbound is a testament to the power of community, resilience, and a steadfast commitment to a creative vision. From the initial sparks of inspiration to the challenges faced and the ongoing development, Heartbound's odyssey is a story that transcends the digital realm, echoing the collaborative spirit that defines the indie gaming landscape.

Part 6

Heartbound's Ongoing Saga: Navigating Monthly Updates, Beta Releases, and the Road Ahead

As the sun continues to rise and set on the development horizon of Heartbound, the journey unfolds with a tapestry of monthly update videos, beta releases, and a gaze toward the future. In this exploration, we delve into the heartbeat of Heartbound's ongoing narrative, examining the significance of monthly updates, the progress made through beta releases, and the roadmap that guides the game toward its future goals.

Monthly Update Videos: A Window into Development

The heartbeat of Heartbound isn't just the rhythm of gameplay; it's the steady cadence of monthly update videos that offer a glimpse behind the digital curtain. Beginning in 2022, these videos became a pivotal channel of communication between the development team at Pirate Software and the dedicated community eagerly anticipating the game's completion.

1. Transparency and Community Engagement:

- Monthly update videos serve as a beacon of transparency, providing a window into the development process. They go beyond mere progress reports, offering insights into the challenges faced, the decisions made, and the evolving vision for Heartbound. This commitment to openness fosters a sense of trust within the community, transforming players into active participants in the game's development journey.

2. Showcasing Progress and Features:

- Each video is a showcase of the progress made in the preceding month. From new gameplay mechanics to narrative developments, the videos serve as a visual chronicle of Heartbound's evolution. Features, improvements, and glimpses into upcoming content create a tapestry of anticipation, keeping the community engaged and invested in the game's growth.

3. Fostering Community Connection:

- The videos are more than just informative updates; they are a means of fostering a connection between the development team and the community. Developers share not only the technical aspects of the game but also their passion, dedication, and sometimes, the challenges faced. This humanizes the development process, creating a shared narrative where players become collaborators in the unfolding story of Heartbound.

Beta Releases and Development Progress

The heartbeat of development is not just heard in the cadence of updates but felt in the pulse of beta releases. These milestones are not just checkpoints; they are pivotal moments that bridge the gap between anticipation and realization, allowing players to step into the evolving world of Heartbound.

1. Beta Version of Chapter 3: "Animus":

- The beta release of Chapter 3, titled "Animus," marked a significant step forward in the Heartbound odyssey. Released on December 24, 2023, this beta version provided players with a taste of the new narrative, challenges, and gameplay mechanics that awaited them. Beta releases are not just about testing; they are about inviting the community to actively participate in shaping the final product.

2. Community Feedback and Iterative Development:
- Beta releases serve as a two-way street. Players dive into the new content, and their experiences, feedback, and bug reports become invaluable data for the development team. This iterative

process ensures that Heartbound is not just a creation of the developers but a collaborative effort where player insights contribute to the refinement and polish of the game.

3. Balancing Expectations and Surprises:

- Beta releases strike a delicate balance between meeting player expectations and offering surprises. While certain elements are teased in advance, the true magic lies in the discovery of uncharted territories within the game. Beta versions are a microcosm of the delicate dance between anticipation and revelation, a dance that keeps the Heartbound community eagerly awaiting each new release.

Future Release Plans and Goals

The future, shrouded in the mists of anticipation, holds both the culmination of the Heartbound journey and the promise of new beginnings. As of the last available information, the full release of Heartbound is slated for 2024. The roadmap is not just a linear path; it's a dynamic itinerary that outlines the vision for the game's future.

1. Chapter Unveilings and Narrative Expansion:
   - The full release of Heartbound isn't merely a conclusion; it's a celebration of the complete narrative experience. Players can expect the unveiling of

subsequent chapters, each adding new layers to the overarching story. The narrative expansion goes hand in hand with the non-linear nature of Heartbound, providing players with multiple pathways and endings to explore.

2. Ongoing Community Engagement:

- The heartbeat of community engagement will continue to echo through the ongoing development. Future updates, whether in the form of additional chapters, features, or optimizations, will be shaped not only by the vision of the development team but also by the vibrant heartbeat of the Heartbound community. This ongoing collaboration ensures that Heartbound remains a living, breathing creation that resonates with the players who have invested their anticipation and support.

3. Post-Release Support and Iterative Development:

- The release of Heartbound is not the end; it's a new beginning. Post-release support and iterative development are integral components of the future plans. Beyond the initial release, the developers aim to address player feedback, introduce optimizations, and potentially expand the Heartbound universe with additional content. The game's future will be a reflection of the ongoing dialogue between the creators and the community.

Evolution and Adaptation: Navigating the Unknown

As with any journey, the future of Heartbound is subject to the unpredictable winds of the development landscape. Challenges may arise, unforeseen opportunities may present themselves, and the game's evolution will continue to be a dynamic process of adaptation. The commitment to transparency and community engagement serves as a compass, guiding Heartbound through the uncharted waters that lie ahead.

In conclusion, Heartbound's updates and future plans are not just waypoints on a map; they are the rhythmic beats that propel the game forward. Monthly update videos, beta releases, and the roadmap for the future are integral components of a journey that extends beyond the digital realm. Heartbound is not just a game; it's an ongoing saga that unfolds in collaboration with a community that shares in the anticipation, challenges, and triumphs of the Heartbound odyssey.

Part 7:

Heartbound's Journey: Navigating the Tides of Reception and Controversies

In the vast sea of indie games, Heartbound embarked on a journey that stirred waves of anticipation, garnered recognition, and even navigated the occasional controversy. This exploration delves into the reception of Heartbound during its alpha and beta phases, the comparisons drawn with the iconic Undertale, and the notable recognition the game achieved on platforms like Game Jolt.

Alpha and Beta Reception: Riding the Waves of Positivity

The initial waves of reception for Heartbound during its alpha and beta phases were not mere ripples; they were resounding echoes of positivity that reverberated through the gaming community. Both IGN and Game Skinny expressed interest in the direction the game was headed, setting the stage for a journey that would be closely watched and eagerly anticipated.

1. IGN and Game Skinny Interest:

- The alpha and beta releases of Heartbound were met with enthusiasm and positive feedback from notable gaming media outlets. IGN, a leading source for gaming news and reviews, acknowledged the potential of Heartbound, indicating that the game had captured the attention of industry observers. Game Skinny, known for its coverage of indie games, also expressed interest, laying the foundation for a growing awareness of Heartbound within the gaming community.

2. Top Indie Release on Game Jolt:

- On October 3, 2018, Heartbound claimed the second spot for the top indie release on Game Jolt. This recognition on a prominent indie gaming platform highlighted the game's appeal and potential, as players flocked to experience the unique narrative and gameplay mechanics offered by Heartbound. The positive reception on Game Jolt became a testament to the game's growing popularity within the indie gaming sphere.

Comparisons with Undertale: Navigating Controversial Waters

As Heartbound set sail on its journey, it inevitably encountered the currents of comparison with Undertale, a game that had left an indelible mark on the indie gaming landscape. Undertale's innovative narrative design, memorable characters, and unconventional approach to player choices had set a high standard. Heartbound, with its thematic similarities and gameplay mechanics, found itself navigating the controversial waters of comparison.

1. Mechanical and Visual Similarities:
- Heartbound's gameplay and visual style drew comparisons with Undertale, leading to discussions and debates within the gaming community. The mechanical similarities, such as the avoidance of random battles and the focus on player choices impacting the narrative, prompted players and critics alike to draw parallels between the two games. The visual aesthetics, while

distinct, carried echoes of the beloved Undertale.

2. Controversies and Confusion:

- The comparisons with Undertale sparked controversies, with some expressing concerns that Heartbound might be perceived as derivative rather than innovative. This controversy extended to popular YouTuber MatPat, known for his game theory content, potentially causing confusion with his coverage of Undertale. While the developers of Heartbound navigated these turbulent waters, they remained steadfast in emphasizing the unique elements and narrative direction that set their game apart.

3. Divergence in Themes and Storytelling:

- Heartbound's narrative, while sharing thematic elements with Undertale, diverged in its storytelling approach. The central narrative of a protagonist dealing with depression, anxiety, and fear on a quest to find his dog, Baron, set Heartbound on a distinct emotional trajectory. The game explored the complexities of mental health and personal growth, weaving a narrative that resonated with players on a deeply emotional level.

Recognition on Game Jolt: Riding the Crests of Success

Amidst the controversies and comparisons, Heartbound continued to ride the crests of success, achieving recognition on Game Jolt. The platform, known for showcasing indie games and fostering a vibrant community, played a significant role in amplifying Heartbound's visibility within the gaming sphere.

1. Top Indie Release:

   - Heartbound's ascent to the top of the indie releases on Game Jolt was a noteworthy achievement. The platform, with its diverse audience of indie game enthusiasts, provided Heartbound with a stage to shine. Claiming the first place in the indie release category on January 1, 2024, marked a symbolic triumph for the game and its journey through the indie gaming landscape.

2. Community Engagement:

- Recognition on Game Jolt wasn't just a numerical accolade; it translated into heightened community engagement. Players on the platform actively participated in discussions, shared their experiences, and contributed to the communal narrative surrounding Heartbound. The recognition on Game Jolt became a testament to the game's ability to resonate with the indie gaming community.

3. Expanding Player Base: - The success on Game Jolt contributed to an expanding player base, as the game reached new audiences eager to explore the emotional depths and unique gameplay offered by Heartbound. The recognition on the platform served as a beacon, guiding players toward a narrative experience that went beyond conventional gaming norms.

Navigating the Waves of Reception: A Conclusion

In conclusion, Heartbound's journey through the tides of reception and controversies is a testament to the game's ability to leave a lasting impact within the indie gaming landscape. The positive reception during its alpha and beta phases, recognition on platforms like Game Jolt, and the controversies surrounding comparisons with Undertale all became integral components of Heartbound's narrative.

As the game continues its voyage toward the full release in 2024, it carries with it the echoes of community engagement, the waves of positive reception, and the resilience to navigate controversies. Heartbound isn't just a game; it's a journey that invites players to explore themes of emotion, choice, and personal growth, creating a narrative tapestry that unfolds within the dynamic currents of the indie gaming sea.

Part 8

Building the Heartbound Guild: Crafting a Community Tapestry

In the vast realm of gaming, the Heartbound Guild stands as more than a mere collective of players; it's a vibrant community woven together by shared enthusiasm for the indie role-playing game, Heartbound. This exploration delves into the intricate threads of community building, unraveling the guild's name and theme, examining the platforms fostering community engagement, and exploring the diverse activities that bind guild members both in and out of the game.

Guild Name and Theme: The Heartbeat of Community Identity

A guild's name is not just a label; it's a resonant echo that encapsulates the essence of the community it represents. The Heartbound Guild, true to its name, is a collective bound by the beating heart of shared passion for the game. The name, carefully chosen, reflects the emotional and narrative depth that Heartbound offers, setting the tone for a community that extends beyond the confines of the game itself.

1. Heartbound Theme:

- The thematic alignment with Heartbound serves as the cornerstone of the guild's identity. The game, revolving around a protagonist's journey through emotions, relationships, and personal growth, provides a rich backdrop for the guild's theme. Members share a common thread of exploring the intricacies of the game's narrative, fostering discussions, theories, and a deep emotional connection to the characters and world of Heartbound.

2. Symbolism and Unity:

- The heart, as a symbol, holds potent connotations of emotion, connection, and resilience. In choosing the heart as a central symbol, the guild emphasizes unity and shared experiences. Each member becomes a vital part of the collective heartbeat, contributing to the overall rhythm and vitality of the Heartbound Guild. The symbolism goes beyond the virtual, creating a sense of belonging that transcends the digital realm.

3. Inclusivity and Community Spirit:

- The Heartbound Guild, through its name and theme, promotes inclusivity and a vibrant community spirit. Members are not just players; they are storytellers, explorers, and guardians of the guild's shared narrative. The theme creates a space where diverse voices and perspectives converge, fostering an environment where everyone feels not just welcomed but essential to the guild's identity.

Community Engagement Platforms: The Nexus of Connection

In the digital age, community building extends beyond the confines of in-game interactions. The Heartbound Guild has embraced a diverse array of platforms, creating a nexus of connection that goes beyond the pixels of the game world.

1. Discord: The Heartbound Hub:
   - Discord stands as the heartbeat of the Heartbound Guild, serving as the central

hub for communication, discussions, and community engagement. Channels dedicated to lore discussions, gameplay strategies, and fan art become virtual spaces where guild members converge. The real-time nature of Discord enhances the sense of immediacy, creating an environment where members can share their experiences, theories, and excitement in the heartbeat of the moment.

2. Social Media Platforms: Extending the Tapestry:

- Beyond the confines of Discord, the Heartbound Guild extends its reach across social media platforms. Twitter, Facebook, and Instagram become canvases where the guild's vibrant tapestry is showcased. From sharing fan art to celebrating milestones and updates, these platforms serve as windows into the Heartbound community, allowing members to connect with a broader audience and contribute to the collective narrative.

3. Streaming and Content Creation: Guild Showcases:

- The Heartbound Guild embraces the dynamic world of streaming and content creation. Members who explore the realms of Twitch, YouTube, or other platforms become guild ambassadors, showcasing their experiences and talents. Whether it's live gameplay sessions, lore discussions, or creative endeavors inspired by Heartbound, these streams and creations become not just individual expressions but threads woven into the larger tapestry of the guild's shared narrative.

In-Game and Out-of-Game Activities: Crafting Bonds Beyond Pixels

Community building extends beyond the pixels of the game, manifesting in a rich tapestry of in-game and out-of-game activities. The Heartbound Guild is not just a collective of players; it's a dynamic community that thrives on diverse interactions.

1. In-Game Quests and Events:

- Within the game itself, the Heartbound Guild organizes in-game quests and events that go beyond the regular gameplay experience. Whether it's coordinating group adventures, tackling challenging quests, or organizing in-game celebrations, these activities become the threads that bind guild members within the digital landscape. The shared experiences within Heartbound's world deepen the connections forged within the guild.

2. Book Clubs and Lore Discussions: Beyond the Game World:

- The Heartbound Guild transcends the boundaries of the game through book clubs and lore discussions. Guild members delve into the narrative intricacies of Heartbound, exploring the lore, characters, and thematic elements. These discussions become intellectual journeys that extend beyond the confines of the game, fostering a shared appreciation for the storytelling nuances that make Heartbound a unique and resonant experience.

3. Community Contests and Challenges: Unleashing Creativity:

- To ignite the sparks of creativity within the guild, the Heartbound community organizes contests and challenges. From fan art competitions to creative writing challenges, these activities become outlets for guild members to express their unique perspectives and talents. The contests not only showcase the diversity within the guild but also celebrate the individual contributions that enrich the overall fabric of the Heartbound community.

Conclusion:

The Living Tapestry of Heartbound's Guild

In conclusion, the Heartbound Guild is more than a collective of players; it's a living tapestry woven from threads of shared passion, creativity, and community spirit. The carefully chosen name and theme echo the emotional depth of the game, providing a thematic anchor for guild members. Platforms like Discord and social media serve as the nexus of connection, allowing the heartbeat of the guild to resonate across digital landscapes.

The guild's activities, both in and out of the game, create a dynamic and vibrant community where members are not just

players but active contributors to the shared narrative. In the Heartbound Guild, every member becomes a storyteller, and every interaction adds a new thread to the evolving tapestry. As the guild continues to thrive, it stands as a testament to the enduring power of community building within the realm of gaming.

Heartbound's Odyssey: A Tapestry Woven with Passion and Resilience

As we draw the curtains on the intricate and emotional journey of Heartbound, it's evident that this indie role-playing game has transcended the confines of mere digital entertainment. From its early inception to the ongoing development saga, Heartbound's odyssey has been a tapestry woven with threads of passion, community resilience, and a commitment to storytelling that extends beyond the boundaries of conventional gaming.

Summary of Heartbound's Journey:

Heartbound's journey commenced with a vision inspired by classics like Secret of Mana, EarthBound, and the Mother series. The game, developed by Pirate Software, garnered swift and overwhelming support on Steam Greenlight in December 2016. This early success laid the foundation for a successful Kickstarter campaign in 2017, with backers contributing not just financially but also becoming integral parts of the Heartbound community.

The decision to embrace Steam Early Access in 2018 marked a crucial chapter, allowing players to embark on the initial chapters of Heartbound's narrative. The game's unique approach to storytelling, player choices, and emotional themes resonated with both players and media outlets, earning positive reviews during alpha and beta releases. Heartbound claimed recognition on platforms like Game Jolt, reaching the summit of the top indie releases.

However, the journey wasn't without its challenges. The extended development, influenced by unforeseen obstacles like the global COVID-19 pandemic, tested the resilience of the development team. Monthly update videos became not just progress reports but a lifeline of communication, reassuring the dedicated community and fostering a sense of trust amidst the uncertainties.

As of the latest available information, the beta version of Chapter 3, titled "Animus," was partially released in December 2023, with the full game release projected for 2024. Heartbound's journey remains an ongoing narrative, a story in the making, with each update and development milestone adding layers to the emotional and immersive experience.

Anticipation for Future Releases:

The future of Heartbound holds a promise that goes beyond the conventional notion of game releases. It embodies the anticipation of a community that has weathered delays, shared in the challenges, and celebrated the triumphs of the development team. The Heartbound Guild, an integral part of this narrative, stands as a living testament to the game's ability to foster vibrant and engaged communities.

The guild, with its carefully chosen name and thematic resonance with Heartbound, reflects the emotional depth and shared experiences within the game. The heartbeat of community engagement platforms, from Discord to social media and streaming channels, ensures that the guild remains a dynamic and interconnected entity beyond the pixels of the game world.

In-game activities, from quests and events to book clubs and lore discussions, create bonds that extend beyond the digital landscape. The Heartbound Guild is not just a collection of players; it's a community of storytellers, artists, and enthusiasts who contribute to the living tapestry of Heartbound's narrative.

As the guild embraces the challenges and triumphs of Heartbound, it becomes a microcosm of the broader community awaiting the future releases. The anticipation extends not just to the next chapters of the game but to the evolving narrative of the Heartbound Guild and the diverse activities that weave its communal tapestry.

The heart, both as a symbol and a thematic anchor, remains at the core of this anticipation. It symbolizes not only the emotional depth explored within Heartbound but also the unity and resilience of a community that beats in sync with the heartbeat of the game.

In conclusion, Heartbound's odyssey is far from over. It's a narrative that unfolds not just within the game's code but in the interactions, stories, and creativity of the community that surrounds it. The anticipation for future releases is not just about the content that awaits; it's about the continuation of a journey that has become a shared experience, a tapestry woven with threads of passion, anticipation, and a collective love for the world of Heartbound. As the story continues to evolve, the community remains an integral part, contributing to a legacy that extends far beyond the digital realm.